Golf

Golf Strategies
The Perfect Swing
Golf Game Preparation

By Ace McCloud
Copyright © 2014

Disclaimer

The information provided in this book is designed to provide helpful information on the subjects discussed. This book is not meant to be used, nor should it be used, to diagnose or treat any medical condition. For diagnosis or treatment of any medical problem, consult your own physician. The publisher and author are not responsible for any specific health or allergy needs that may require medical supervision and are not liable for any damages or negative consequences from any treatment, action, application or preparation, to any person reading or following the information in this book. Any references included are provided for informational purposes only. Readers should be aware that any websites or links listed in this book may change.

Table of Contents

Introduction 6
Chapter 1: The Origins of Golf 7
Chapter 2: The Perfect Swing 9
Chapter 3: Strategies and Secrets 21
Chapter 4: Physical and Mental Preparation 26
Chapter 5: Exercise, Nutrition and Supplements 30
Chapter 6: Equip Yourself for Success 37
Conclusion 42
My Other Books and Audio Books 44

Be sure to check out my website for all my Books and Audio books.

www.AcesEbooks.com

Introduction

I want to thank and congratulate you for buying the book: "Golf Secrets, Tips, And Strategies Revealed: How to get the perfect swing, How to prepare for the game, and how to use top golfing strategies used by pros."

This book contains proven steps and strategies on how to prepare for a game of golf; how to get the perfect swing, how to prepare mentally and secrets that the pros use to succeed.

If you've already tried researching golf strategies, then you may be understandably frustrated with the sheer volume of information and often conflicting advice. This book sums up the most important things that you need to know in order to dramatically improve your golf game. Stop doing what doesn't work and start using the proven strategies that will see you steadily improving day after day and game after game!

Chapter 1: The Origins of Golf

Golf is a remarkable sport that can be played for fun or as a backdrop to mega-business deals. It can be expensive or done very cheaply. It can be world-class competitive or a casual Saturday pastime with friends. Tournaments can have millions in prizes, and games between leaders can help end wars.

Golf levels the playing field in a way that no other sport can. You don't have to be the biggest or the fastest to succeed. The game is played by the young and the old, the fit and the physically challenged. Golf has a universal appeal with a history that goes way back.

The beginnings are hard to pinpoint because people have played with balls and clubs for centuries. Sports enjoyed by ancient Romans have things in common with later Celtic games and much later, hockey. Variations of golf were played throughout Europe in the middle Ages, with evidence that it was popular in Holland. When a sport has been around this long, rules gradually set in over time, but for golf, ways of playing were different in different places. But the one thing they all had in common was hitting a ball from one place to another

In Scotland, "gowf" got banned on Sundays because young soldiers were playing the game instead of honing archery skills. Scotland is credited with developing the modern game. That was around the year 1744 in St. Andrews.

Over the years the sport has gained in popularity tremendously, particularly because it is so inclusive to all types of people of all ages. It is a game that can be played late into life, and all the walking is great exercise and very rarely do people get injured while playing. With major tournaments that offer massive cash prizes being broadcast on the big television channels, the sport is just increasing in popularity. The super stars of the sport, such as Phil Mickelson and Tiger Woods, have also done a lot to make golf even more appealing to a broad audience, bringing in even more fans than ever.

Golf is now a worldwide powerhouse sport, and with its popularity comes an intense desire by many to be able to play it well and master the game. Since golf is an extremely social game, it can get very competitive, and it can be quite enjoyable to beat your friends, colleagues, and fellow competitors. The goal of this book is to give you as much helpful advice as possible so that you can gain as much satisfaction and joy as possible from the game. So let's get started with the perfect golf swing.

Chapter 2: The Perfect Swing

The swing is golf's Holy Grail. If everyone could swing well, then everyone would have a chance to play on pro golfing tours. Hitting a ball across the landscape seems simple enough, but in fact, golf is quite complex and requires a good amount of knowledge. Mastering the swing is the main thing needed to be good at the game. As is required for competence in any sport; golf demands patience, practice and focus.

Unlike other sports that involve striking balls, the golf ball will not be moving when you need to hit it, and just one major swing needs to be mastered. To get the perfect swing, it is vitally important to learn how to hit the ball in the center of the club.

Debate rages about which is more important, mastering putting or swinging straight and hard on the fairways. Experts say that 40 percent of a golf score is earned from putting. On the other hand, the driving distances of pro golfers are far greater than those of amateurs.

Most instructors will tell you a lot of specific things to do with your body in order to execute a proper swing. The problem is, trying to remember and carry out all the steps is nearly impossible. For most beginners, attempting to learn this way makes the swing worse. The steps involve variations of turning shoulders, hips, and shifting weight. These tips are technically correct in that the body does have to be aligned and move in certain ways to execute the best shot. The key is being able to swing in the most natural and efficient manner possible without having to memorize and focus on the 'proper' steps. For most people, this type of mechanical instruction is just too complex and distracting.

One problem is that everyone's body is different, so the perfect natural swing is slightly different for everyone. It can even be said that a person's swing reflects their personality.

A golf swing is a lot like a baseball bat swing except the ball is not at waist level. The first part of the swing is preparation, and then the actual swing. A pre-shot routine for most people involves a practice swing to one side of the ball. Then the actual swing should be a fluid, circular motion around the body.

Golf swings can vary quite a bit. There are those who play by feel and those who like to take a strict mechanical approach. Golfers who play purely by feel care little about some of the more technical aspects of a golf swing, preferring to do what just comes naturally to them. 'Mechanics,' on the other hand, like to think of the swing as a procedure of steps that they try to follow precisely each time.

On a scale of one to ten, with one being feel-based and 10 being totally mechanical, here's how some pros fit in: Tiger Woods, Vijay Singh and Annika Sorenstam (the world's top female golfer) are all around a number five on the scale, using feel and mechanics to get their perfect swing. Phil Mickelson and Sergio Garcia, on the other hand, consider themselves one or two on the scale, preferring to go almost totally by feel and natural instinct.

So which approach is best? As you may have figured out by now - neither. But keep reading to learn which direction this guide (and the experts) lean toward for most people.

Golf Swing Tips:

Beware of golf swing fads. There aren't any new types of swings that top golfers just started using.

The most important tip is to **relax** your body. Being angry or upset at anything can ruin not just your swing, but possibly even your entire round. It is important to stay calm and relaxed. If you find yourself getting angry or frustrated then you will need to take the appropriate steps to get your head back into the game. We will go into this in more detail later in the book.

The **less you think** about the swing, the better it will be. Again, this may take a lot of practice. Overthinking creates tension which can be very detrimental to your game. The fact that there are huge gaps of time between shots does not help those with active minds and tendencies to over-think, so instead of using that time to beat yourself up, use it more appropriately to prepare yourself for your next shot. Visualize yourself making the perfect swing, the crowd roaring, and everyone wanting your autograph. Imagine yourself holding the victory trophy or the feeling that you will get when you have just made an incredible putt. Stay away from negativity as much as possible. You need to have a winner's mentality, and winners don't whine or cry or complain or quit when the going gets tough. Everyone likes a good comeback story, so even if things don't start out the way you want, don't give up, and practice your ability to turn things around!

Another strategy many pros will use is to chant an empowering phrase to themselves in their head while they are heading for their next swing or putt. This can be anything that helps get you in the proper frame of mind. For example: "I'm a champion, I always win, I make the most incredible shots and my putts always go in." You just repeat this in your head over and over, allowing no other thoughts to come in. Now imagine how much better your next golf swing will be if you spent the last ten minutes chanting this phrase in your head and visualizing yourself making perfect shots all the way to the end of the course. I know this can be difficult and can require a lot of discipline and willpower, so if this is something you would seriously like to improve upon, then I would highly recommend you read my book on: Influence, Willpower, and Discipline.

Get a Grip:

First, rest the head of the club on the ground. For left-handed swingers, reverse the following directions: Grip the club near the top with your left hand like you're shaking hands with it. Place your thumb pointing downward at the grip's front end. Now use a similar grip with your right hand, below your left hand and again with that thumb pointing downward at the grip's front end. Many golfers then intertwine their right-hand baby finger with their left index finger for a more unified feel, but go with whatever is most comfortable to you.

Grip pressure is very important in the stress of a competitive match. Nervous golfers tend to hold onto the club too tightly and that almost always rules out a smooth swing. Lightening up on the club's grip will allow the swing to be more stable.

Body Positioning and the Actual Swing:

Your stance is the foundation; it is what the rest of the swing flows from. Consistency is a significant part of the game. Once you have a stance that is comfortable and which works, try doing it the same way each time.

In golf talk, the point where you align your feet and shoulders with the target is called 'addressing the ball.'

Line up your toes so that if you set a club down alongside them, they would point to the target. Stand three feet behind the ball and then find a spot about three feet in front of the ball that is lined up towards where you want the ball to go. Keep your eyes on that spot and then move beside the ball, lining up your body and club. Next, plant your feet and make sure that the same amount of weight presses on your heels and on the balls of your feet. In other words, try and balance in-between, on your arches. Be sure to keep the same amount of weight on your left foot as your right foot so that it is evenly distributed.

After all that, it's now okay to lean forward a bit and swing with a fluid motion. Pretending that the club head is really heavy helps keep your arms straight and allows the club head to take the lead, helping swing your body around the right way. This also contributes to an unbroken and smooth swinging motion.

If you're making a solid connection with the ball but it regularly goes to the left or the right, it can mean your body is not properly aligned or that your feet are not lined up precisely enough with the direction the ball is supposed to go. Poor alignment can creep back into the game very easily, even for veterans.

Swing strength and distance will come with practice, and so will the swing's smoothness, which will help improve your accuracy. Think of the long-term goal when you are at the practice range – not about your next game, but rather how your game will be significantly improved over the next few months and years by the work you are putting in now.

Keep in mind that about half of all strokes take place close to the hole, usually within 50 or 60 yards. This means it would be wise to spend more of your practice time with wedges and the putter. Most golfers do not do this.

Putting

Putting is not the game's most showy aspect, but that does not mean the putt should be overlooked. Too often, this important part of the game is an afterthought.

Freeing the mind for a good putt is more difficult when under duress. So if you had a hard time getting to the green in the first place due to bad shots, it can sometimes be extremely difficult to relax and get yourself in the proper frame of mind. Do your best to relax and maintain your composure. Even the best in the world blow putts they should have been able to easily sink on national TV, so don't beat yourself up too bad if this happens to you, just use the mental techniques mentioned earlier to get your brain back on track.

The only 'mechanical' thing of importance when putting is to make sure that you strike the ball in the middle of the face of the putter, square on, and not from any other angle. Where the club face points at the moment of impact is the sole thing that determines ball direction.

Putting tips:

When putting, you want a long and flowing stroke. The best way to accomplish that is by standing tall. A taller stance is liberating, allowing the arms to make a smooth and flowing motion. Standing tall also encourages the knees and hips to assist ever-so-slightly with the stroke.

Think about rolling the ball, rather than hitting it. This mental trick helps with distance control. Another trick for freeing the mind is to avoid staring at the ball. Staring can result in a bad putt. Try looking at a spot in front of the ball on the target line. Focusing on the target line helps to keep your mind off of the stroke. Also, when you're quite a distance away from the hole, concentrate on a three-foot circle around the hole to help improve your putting accuracy.

When putting, make sure your fingers are in contact with the grip. It is your fingers rather than palms which are crucial to feel, and when putting you will perform much better if you can feel the shot. Putting requires more feel and less mechanics than other golf shots.

To see a great putting video by Gary Player, a top golfer who is considered by many to be the world's best putter, watch this YouTube video: <u>Gary Player Putting Tips</u> posted by Odyssey Golf. It is important to remember that all techniques are not going to be perfect for every person. You will need to experiment to find out what works best for you. Don't make the mistake of practicing one technique for months or even years at a time, when a little research and experimentation could have found you a much better technique that is more suited to you and that would dramatically improve your gameplay. Do this research and experimentation for all aspects of the game and your game will be significantly better for many years to come. Remember, every person is different, and things that work great for one person, will not necessarily work great for you. Try and match your play style with your personality, and remember, when it comes to golf, one size definitely does not fit all.

In Bunkers and the Rough

Many golfers have trouble getting out of sand traps because they don't take a full swing. They worry about hitting the ball out too far, but what will tend to happen is they will not hit the ball hard enough to escape the trap. Be sure to take a full swing as there is a sand cushion which often helps ensure the ball doesn't travel too far.

A few years ago Tiger Woods admitted needing work ON playing the bunkers. "Sand saves not only help you maintain momentum," he said, "they can give you a real mental boost in the heat of competition. Because bunker shots are as much feel as proper technique, I worked really hard on the part where feel is critical…to control distance."

As with other golf instruction that delves into technicalities of the swing, opinion on the best way to get out of bunkers is not unanimous. Some experts recommend using your lower body when chipping. In other words, pivot the hips to add some rhythm. Others recommend keeping the lower body still.

Choosing the right club to get out of a bunker can be tricky. Pick an iron that's one number above the one you think you need. It's a conservative strategy. But unless you're a geometry expert, you may hit the bunker lip with, say, a seven iron, when you should have chosen the nine. The nine of course will not take the ball as far, but the added lift (called loft in golf) will get you out of the bunker.

In the rough, do not swing your wedges as hard as you can. Doing so risks poor contact and wild shots. If you're in grass that's an inch or more deep, tighten the grip on your club to keep it from twisting.

Golf pros note that course designers in recent years have exhibited a sadistic streak by making courses with more rough areas, and making those areas rougher than ever. The best thing for improving scores is getting back on the fairway as quickly as possible.

Tempo is a marker of consistency. Try keeping the same tempo with each swing. If you execute a really bad shot during a round in which you had many other great swings, it could be due to your tempo getting too fast. This often takes place at a crucial time in the game, so slow down.

Practice your swing and when you start making good shots, practice some more and keep up the good habits. As your swing becomes consistent, then so will your game.

Watch Golf Videos

Golf videos on sites like YouTube can be very helpful because the game is visually-oriented. Just remember that you are going to have to develop your own unique swing. While Phil Mickelson is one of the best golfers in the world, his swing is tailored for his strengths and does not work well for everyone. Be sure to experiment and find a swing that works best for you, and watching the swings of others can give you some great ideas. Once you have found out what works best for you, practice that swing consistently.

[Top 10 Phil Mickelson Shots](#) by the PGA Tour
[Phil Mickelson Waste Management Open 2013](#) by Bernard Sheridan

For beginners, the most elegant swing to watch is Tiger Woods'. As with the other champion golfers, armchair and pro analysts online are obsessed with changes to his swing. Here is a classic Tiger Woods' swing on slow motion video:

[Tiger Woods' Swing](#) by jael95

This is a great demonstration of what is considered to be the world's best perfect swing.

Chapter 3: Strategies and Secrets

It's amazing how many golfers swing by looking at the ball without any reference towards the hole. You want to take several hard looks at exactly where you want the ball to go just before you swing. Other books love to go into great detail of countless steps, intricate body mechanics and physical theories of the golf swing that 99% of people will not remember or will find nearly impossible to emulate.

There are just two things about the swing that you really need to remember. It is divided into two parts. The upswing is when you start out by swinging the club up over your head. Then there's the downswing, the part when you strike the ball. Any more breaking down of the golf swing, I'm afraid, will descend into an instructional abyss of memorization and confusion.

Now that we've isolated the backswing, here's a great tip: No need to rush the backswing, you're not hitting the ball with it. In fact, a very slow start to the backswing is a secret to a more controlled swing overall. Most experts advise against stopping at the top of the backswing, because the momentum of not stopping loads up the muscles with more power. But other experts point out that while power may be gained this way; stopping has benefits like greater consistency and sense of control. Less muscle strain and fewer injuries are also reported. So try it both ways and choose what works best for you.

Here's another great downswing tip: think fast, not hard. When you try to swing too hard there is a lot of tension, which is not wanted. A quick and fluid swing will be extremely powerful, so focus on the speed of your swing.

Try setting up guides that will help with alignment: lay down clubs along the line of flight that you want. It helps if you have an attitude about not caring what other people think. Self-conscious learners may want to book a range time for off-peak hours.

Try not to put too much focus on hitting every shot perfectly, nobody can do that, and it just leads to frustration. Golf is about continuous adjustment. A good approach is to try and minimize the negative effects of a bad shot when you do hit one.

Develop a routine on the practice range. Don't start with rip-roaring drives. As tempting as that will be, it throws off your tempo. Instead, begin with a wedge or low-numbered iron. Move to the middle irons and then work toward using the wood drivers.

Monitor your progress. Bring a notebook with you when playing and keep track of what happened and what club you were using when you made your good shots and your bad shots. Also, keep track in your notebook or golf diary other factors as well that can help you in the future. Did you have a lot of energy this particular day? What where you're eating habits leading up to the game that contributed to this increase in energy? What type of mood where you in throughout the game? Keep track of all the information you can think of, then after several months you should be able to go back and analyze this diary and be able to come up with a strategic routine that works well for you that you should follow consistently in the future to obtain your desired results on the golf course.

A good golf mentor really helps. This should be someone you like and trust, and of course who is a really good golfer. They can help with both the physical and mental aspect of the game. A good mentor or instructor can see what's going wrong first hand and give you valuable advice to help you improve your game.

One aspect of golf not yet mentioned is called course management, or fairway play. In short, it means playing strategy. For example, if a bunker is blocking your clear shot to the hole, then you need to decide what strategy to take in order to be the most effective. You can boldly decide that now is the moment when ten yards can suddenly be added to your drive and try to shoot over the bunker. Another option is choosing a club that you're pretty sure will make the ball fall just short of the bunker, which would be a safer shot and lessen your chances of a really terrible round. Maybe you can hit the ball to the left or right of the bunker to optimize your chances. Experts usually advise taking the most direct route, but you need to have a strategy in place that suits your talents and play style. Also, if you are playing a friend and you are way ahead of them, it may be wiser to choose a safer route, on the other hand, if you need to gain ground, you can try being more aggressive to try and catch up. Either strategy can backfire, so it's usually best to just play your game and make each shot as effective as possible.

Here's another fairway play strategy, especially for beginners: When shooting for the green (called an approach shot), aim for its middle no matter the contours or location of the flag. The goal is simply to start putting, period.

If these golf tips and recommendations seem a little conservative that's because, well, they are. Time has proven that a conservative strategy works best for low scores. You don't see top golfers taking bold risks. With every shot, note where the worst trouble is and play away from it

Don't over-think your strategy decisions. Keep it simple and once a decision is made, don't second-guess it, because what you should be doing at this point is focusing on the task at hand. Once on the course, be sure to analyze everything around you, make a decision and go for it to the best of your abilities, trying to stay positive with a clear and focused frame of mind

In order to play your best golf, you have to pick the right shots. And those right shots are the ones you can hit consistently over and over. Play to your strengths and do not think of anything other than hitting the ball in front of you to where you want it to go.

Chapter 4: Physical and Mental Preparation

If you decide to take golf seriously, then you need to make a significant time commitment, and develop your own organized process to maximize your success potential. Mustering the willpower to improve your game will go a long way. Most golfing books and professional instructors are geared toward getting you up and running in a short time frame. This is because it's what everyone actually wants – to learn instantly. So these methods barely cover the basics and they rarely suggest approaching the sport with a longer-term point of view.

The mental aspect of the game is vastly under-stated. It's mentioned a lot in passing but tutorials rarely go into details. The truth is that golf is the most challenging mentally of any sport. In one study, 90 percent of golfers stated that the mental game was vitally important to their success. However, just 15 percent of the same respondents said that they had not done anything specific to develop their golfing mental skills. If you want to really improve your game, then this is something to focus on along with your training.

You think you feel pressure playing at the local clubhouse tournament. Golf professionals have large audiences with hundreds of thousands of people watching them on TV, announcers scrutinizing their every movement, and untold pressures from friends, family members, coaches, and friends. Not to mention the fact that a bad day could cost them hundreds of thousands of dollars. Believe it or not, pros get the jitters too but they take ownership of that nervousness and make it work for them, most of the time. No professional wants to have TV clips showing them missing the shot to win the tournament broadcast around the world. Being able to cope with pressure will be one of the keys to your success.

Confidence is a very important attribute in determining golf winners and it helps reduce the effects of a pressure filled moment. The game's mental aspects cannot be overstated. Can you guess what improves confidence more than anything? That's right, practice. When you've trained harder than the next guy, you'll not simply feel more confident, that confidence boost will be justified because you will actually be better.

The latest research is indicating that the mental part of the game is more important than the technical process of learning the correct techniques. Being too mechanical can be more of a liability than an asset. Pay attention to things like stance and alignment only at the start of each shot, and then shift gears to begin focusing on the target. You don't want to be devoid of all emotion, as your emotional drive can ratchet up intensity in a positive way.

As for preparing for a golf round, start well in advance. Since dehydration is a common problem, keep hydrated, starting two or even three days beforehand. Drink plenty of water throughout the days and into the evenings.

People tend to under-estimate the physical toll golf can take on you. Don't forget you'll be out there for four or more hours and walking around four to five miles. Be sure that you are warming up properly and stretching to avoid injury. It's nowhere near as fun or effective to play when your back is aching or your legs are hurting from a nagging injury.

On game day, get up really early and have a hearty breakfast. Forget about the Fruit Loops. An apple and a few hardboiled eggs is a good choice. This combination is great for reaching and maintaining good blood sugar levels because of the blend of proteins and complex carbohydrates. Forget about the coffee too. It's a diuretic and it's best to stay hydrated. Have water or Gatorade instead.

Arrive at the course extra early and hit the putting range first. Don't try long putts because you don't want to start missing and get frustrated. Start off easy to help build up your confidence. Next, practice some drives. After fifteen minutes or so you can put yourself under a bit of pressure deliberately. Pretend 'this swing counts,' that it's for a million dollars and to win the tournament. Under pressure in real games, golfers tend to speed up and swing too fast. So be sure to focus on your tempo and rhythm so you don't swing too fast later on. These two things are related to balance, so keep this in mind when making your swing.

It is also a good idea to turn your pre-game practice into a routine. Get in the habit of doing the same things over and over. Over time, you should have your pre-game routine down to a science. Also, don't forget to add visualization to this process. Visualizing a shot just before doing it is just like actually hitting the shot and it is something nearly all the best in the world do.

Just before tee off it's a good idea to drink some more water, about half a liter. For a mid-round snack, just say no to the beer and hot dog the others may be having. Instead, every three or four holes munch on some trail mix or nuts, such as almonds. Fruit is also good, as is turkey jerky. Jerky is loaded with proteins that feed the brain and help with concentration.

When the round is finished, have two more glasses of water and eat some protein to repair muscle damage and replace stored energy that was used up. So by all means treat yourself to a nice steak along with some veggies.

Chapter 5: Exercise, Nutrition and Supplements

We just discussed some good ideas for what to eat before, during and after play. But for the bigger picture, you want to eat well and exercise over the long term. First and foremost, you want to eat properly and get fit for your own benefit, whether or not you're going to take golf seriously. It's a lifestyle choice that pays huge dividends.

You hear about 'off-season' in sports like football and baseball, which correctly implies athletes in those and other sports have a lot of time off. For some people, too much time. The best pro golfers like Tiger Woods, train all year round. His workouts can last for hours and he eats right. Woods sticks to lean meat and seafood, and plenty of fruits and vegetables. No junk food. A classic breakfast for this champion consists of vegetables and egg whites. Lunch and dinners are typically fish or grilled chicken, along with veggies and a salad.

It is important to be in relatively good shape for golf, and to have good strength in a variety of muscles used for the swing. Even though golf can be for almost everyone, those with a decent level of fitness will not be so sore after 18 holes. Golfing a lot while being out of shape can cause pain in the back, shoulders, knees and hips. Golf is especially known for causing back injuries and golfer's elbow. These ailments can destroy a golf season, maybe even two. If you would like to know how to rehab back injuries or just keep your back strong and healthy so you don't get injuries, then be sure to check out my book: Back Pain Cure.

Fitness also reduces fatigue. You've heard repeatedly here that golf is a mental game. Fatigue will cause you to lose focus and your competitive edge.

The golf swing is a blazing, rapid-fire moment. As previously mentioned, it can be compared to a baseball bat swing. Doing that a lot is hard on the body. In some sports they say 'it's all in the wrist.' But not golf. A powerful swing improves scores, big time.

Key muscles used in the golf swing are in the wrist, forearm, shoulders, torso, leg hamstrings and calves. It turns out that many exercises that golfers perform work the wrong muscle groups. This has a negative impact on swing mechanics. For example, heavy resistance exercises leading to excessive muscle bulk can restrict movements needed for a proper swing.

The basic **standing squat** is an example of an effective golf exercise because it works on the legs, hips and mid-section. To do squats, keep your feet planted on the ground, extend arms and move down toward the ground like you're going to sit. Hold it for a moment before going back up. The longer you hold it, the harder the exercise gets. To get a bit more advanced, do this while standing on your toes. Regular squats will strengthen legs to enable more power behind your shots, and will also help prevent injury.

Jogging is a great exercise that can really have a positive impact on golf scores. In addition to the usual benefits like being able to jog anytime and anywhere with no equipment, jogging improves overall body tolerance to help get you through 18 holes. Jogging also strengthens the lower body. Running too much though risks spinal and joint stress, tight hamstrings and even foot problems. A good routine for golfers involves jogging short distances broken up by stretching sessions.

Walking is incredible exercise and can be quite enjoyable. Just like you will be walking all the time on the golf course, you can walk outside and get some fresh air. Walking is a great time to practice your visualization, practice your breathing, and chant positive affirmations to yourself silently. Also it is pretty easy to get yourself motivated to take a leisurely walk and there is almost no chance of injury while walking.

Bicycling is good as well for the same reasons as jogging, and also comes with the same advice about over-doing it.

Swimming is considered excellent for its low impact on joints, and for the fact it encourages good trunk rotation. The water resistance strengthens muscle areas used in golf. The only caution here is to avoid swimming immediately before golfing – the overhead arm motions can affect swing movement patterns during play.

Try this **balance exercise**: Stand so your head all the way down to heels are against a wall. With arms spread apart, bend the elbows while attempting to keep hands, arms and back on the wall. Hold the position for 15 to 20 seconds.

Another great way to improve your balance and overall fitness is with a <u>Confidence Vibration Fitness Machine</u>. I didn't know about this type of machine until my father had hip surgery and it was recommended to him by his doctor to help in the recovery process. All I can say is this machine is awesome! I bought one for myself and love to use it several times a day, especially in the morning's right after I wake up. It sends powerful vibrations through your body that help loosen your muscles, increase strength, and improve balance.

The standing twist with golf club will help develop your core. This will help generate more swing power. With feet apart hip-wide, grasp a golf club chest-high. Slowly move it back and forth.

Heel raises develop muscles in the lower back. This exercise will help by increasing swing power. Stand looking towards a wall, while placing one hand on it. Now raise both heels up – gently – and return them to the ground.

Flexibility could be the most important aspect of fitness when it comes to improving golf ability, because power stems from flexibility. Being flexible makes possible a greater range of movements. That in turn paves the way for extending strength potential.

Here is a good flexibility exercise: **Lie down with arms spread out. While lifting both legs with knees bent at a 90-degrees, breathe in and move them to the right. Breathe out while moving your legs back to the start position. Now reverse it by moving to the left. Go about ten times in each direction. Keep shoulders on the floor while doing this exercise. This exercise is designed to help the shoulders, hips and spine become more flexible.**

As with eating habits, exercise is a personal lifestyle choice. Since everybody has a different body that responds in different ways to different types of fitness regimens, pro golfers recommend sticking with whatever works best for you. If you're not sure, try them all out until you find what suits you best. And don't forget to mix things up a bit and have some fun. An occasional round of tennis, skiing or whatever, fends of boredom and keeps different muscle groups guessing. If you would like to learn more about optimum health and keeping your body healthy and strong, then I would highly recommend you read my bestselling book: Anti-Aging Cure.

Supplements

Most experts agree that following the diet and exercise tips we've talked about will eliminate any need to take supplements. But in the real world, almost all of us falter in attempts to fend off junk food and eat balanced meals all the time. Some supplements, minerals and vitamins may help with fitness and focus. Although this is a complex issue, I can tell you that I have personally had great health results from regularly taking vitamins and minerals since the age of fifteen years old. Do not take any of these without consulting with a doctor or at least a nutritionist.

A few supplements are specifically designed for golfers to help them prepare, replenish during, or recuperate after a round. One popular golf supplement is called Golf Focus. These capsules contain gingko, vitamin B and omega-3 from fish oils. Studies reveal that the mineral phosphatidylserine can accelerate healing and fend off sore muscles. ALR Industries offers an amino-acid based supplement endorsed by golf pro Jeff Rangel. The company says its ingredients decrease the body's production of stress hormones. Whey Protein Isolate offer amino acids, low lactose and 90 percent protein by weight.

Don't forget vitamins that can be purchased over the counter, such as vitamin B12 for boosting energy. Tiger Woods endorses a Gatorade line of drinks that contains theanine. The additive helps golfers concentrate during play. Woods also signed on to endorse Fuse Science supplements, which involves rubbing on your skin a lotion packed with vitamins and electrolytes. The company offers the same concentration in two liquid drops which are taken under the tongue. And finally, my favorite concentration supplement is Focus Formula! I take this nearly every day and you can get it fairly inexpensively.

Chapter 6: Equip Yourself for Success

Did you know you can buy golf clubs individually, the same way the pros do? At thrift stores, they're about a dollar each. Okay okay, so the pros don't buy them at thrift stores. While they buy clubs individually, they're custom-made.

Phil Mickelson and some other pros configure different clubs as they go along. Mickelson has a collection of shafts and club heads that click together with a wrench. He interchanges the pieces to create the exact club that he wants for any given situation. His fine-tuned choices are based on things like course firmness and weather conditions.

Of course you're aware that clubs are available in a wide variety of models, prices and sizes. You should also know that buying a set endorsed by the likes of Sergio Garcia or Rory McIlroy won't improve your game. Buy a set that fits your budget. Even if that means the thrift store, because high quality clubs can often be found there.

Most beginner and intermediate golfers will buy a full set of matching clubs. They include numbers 1, 3 and 5 woods; seven irons or hybrids, a pitching wedge and putter. The advantage of matching clubs is that each will have a similar feel. Sets are also the most cost-effective way to purchase, especially since a bag is often included. A decent set can cost under $200.

Golf rules say you can carry 14 clubs, so there's room for two more if you decide down the road that you want more. Some pro golfers recommend using just ten clubs, especially for beginners. Having a small number of clubs creates a sharper focus and more opportunity to master each one.

You'll have to choose between regular and stiff flex. The stiff shafts are for those with faster and more aggressive swings. A few turns on a driving range with each type is the best way to determine the best fit. It will be the flex type that feels easier to control.

Use the woods for driving off the tee and for long fairway shots. They're no longer made of real wood, but metal.

Irons are used on fairways for every shot except the furthest-distance ones that you used the wood ones for.

Hybrids combine advantages of irons with the more forgiving nature of woods. Players have traditionally found irons one through four hard to hit because of their low trajectory and small heads. So they'd use woods instead. But those are not so good where the fairway is rough. Their swing personalities are most suitable for tee shots. You can buy your golf set with hybrids instead of irons, but for most people, the best option would be starting out with the standard irons.

After gaining experience, many golfers replace irons one through four with hybrids. They are designed more for getting the ball in the air, which is perfect for thick grass and other rough places your ball could end up.

Pitching wedges are used on short shots closer to the green. They cause the ball to go high and spin.

Putters of course are used on the greens. It'll be your most-used club.

Many top pro golfers use the Callaway brand, and as luck would have it the company offers top-rated consumer-level sets. The Callaway Strata 13-piece set and bag, for example, costs around $200. For that price you get graphite shafts with a light flex. One hundred dollars more can purchase a Wilson Golf Profile HL Long Set. Also highly rated is the 15-piece Wilson set which is engineered for those with faster swing speeds. The bag features a nifty built-in stand that folds out, so it doesn't have to lay flat on the links. In addition to looking better aesthetically, a bag standing upright avoids a lot of bending over.
If you are looking for a powerful driver then the Taylor Made r11 is very nice and so is the Callaway X Hot Driver.

It's also very nice to have the proper shoes. Most beginners don't go out and buy spiked golf shoes right away, but for those who decide to commit to the game

- and to yet another expense – proper golf shoes will improve balance and direct more energy into the swing. Ones with proper fit and support can also help prevent pain in the lower back, hips and knees. A good pair will usually cost about one hundred dollars.

The last things you'll need of course are balls. Just starting out, you're probably going to lose plenty of them. Predictably enough, the recommendation here is to not buy the most expensive ones. As you start cutting down on ball losses, it makes sense to graduate upwards to the next price level. One way to compare different ball brands is by putting. As you putt, try to detect different feels the balls have. If you would like the number one balls in golf then checkout the Titleist Pro V1 Golf Balls.

Golf Swing Aids

Many golf aids appear attractive as shortcuts, but do they work? Some new ones may, for those who lean toward the mechanical approach to learning the swing. Technology has made possible smartphone apps that do a pretty good job at analyzing your swing. Since you may be taking your device out on the course anyway, you might give the new technology a try. The apps come with small 3-D motion sensors which attach to your club. They send swing data to your phone. Data recordings that you review later will analyze things like swing speed, alignment, shape of the swing arc, tempo and club face angle. Some brand names are In the Swing, Swingbyte, 3BaysGSA Pro, GolfSense 3D, and SwingTIP. They range in price between $130 and $250.

Other golf aid devices, besides the actual equipment itself, usually do not have that great an impact on gameplay, but this will also depends on the type of person you are and the type of game you play. It is generally best to invest in the actual equipment you will be using and to spend more time eating healthy, exercising, and practicing.

Conclusion

Please remember that each golfer has different strengths and weaknesses. For some it's the drive while others may need to work on putting. And then there is the often-neglected chipping and wedge shots. The sooner you learn personal weaknesses, the faster you can focus practice sessions on fixing the problems.

You've been learning the importance of the mental game. People's minds react in unique ways to different circumstances, and each golf game presents different circumstances. Learn how you react under pressure and device strategies that work best for you so that you can thrive under this pressure.

The next step is to practice. A lot. Go to a driving range and set up something for putting in your garage, home office or den. Get to know your local courses. Pick a favorite club and get a membership. Go golfing with your friends or family members. After golfing for a while, soon enough your strengths and weak spots will reveal themselves. Pros zoom in on weakness and spend considerable time (and money) fixing flaws. So for beginners, it becomes simply a matter of how much time (and money) you're willing to invest towards a better score.

Above all, remember that golf is meant to be fun. It's a game, not a life and death thing. Believe in your abilities and your potential.

Finally, if you discovered at least one thing that has helped you or that you think would be beneficial to someone else, be sure to take a few seconds to easily post a quick positive review. As an author, your positive feedback is desperately needed. Your highly valuable five star reviews are like a river of golden joy flowing through a sunny forest of mighty trees and beautiful flowers! *To do your good deed in making the world a better place by helping others with your valuable insight, just leave a nice review.*

My Other Books and Audio Books
www.AcesEbooks.com

Peak Performance Books

Health Books

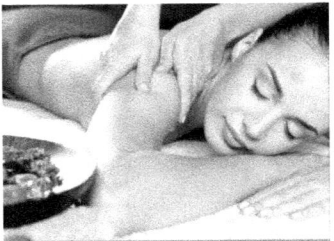

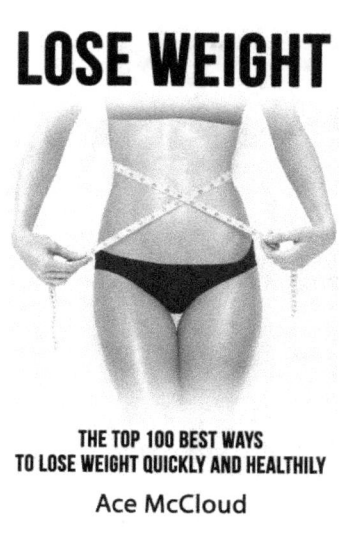 

Be sure to check out my audio books as well!

 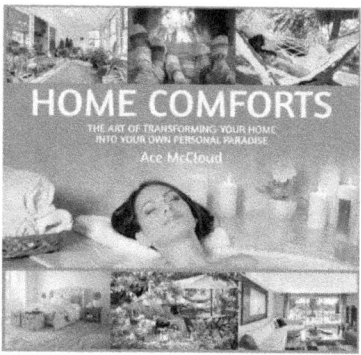 

Check out my website at: **www.AcesEbooks.com** for a complete list of all of my books and high quality audio books. I enjoy bringing you the best knowledge in the world and wish you the best in using this information to make your journey through life better and more enjoyable! **Best of luck to you!**

www.ingramcontent.com/pod-product-compliance
Lightning Source LLC
Chambersburg PA
CBHW051425070526
44584CB00023B/3587